Venus

Earth

Asteroid Belt

Saturn

Neptune

A Look at
Pluto

A Look at Pluto

Salvatore Tocci

Franklin Watts

A DIVISION OF SCHOLASTIC INC.
NEW YORK · TORONTO · LONDON · AUCKLAND
SYDNEY · MEXICO CITY · NEW DELHI · HONG KONG
DANBURY, CONNECTICUT

FOR PATTI,
*whose constant support and encouragement
enabled me to convey to readers what I once conveyed
to students: Although much has been learned in science,
much more remains to be discovered.*

Photographs © 2003: AP/Wide World Photos/Beth A. Keiser: 78; Corbis Images/UPI: 79; Getty Images/Jason Reed: cover; Lowell Observatory: 55 (Marc Buie), 16, 19, 32; Mary Evans Picture Library: 21; NASA: 76 (G. Bacon/STSI), 2, 52, 64, 69, 71, 101, 107; New Mexico State University Library/Rio Grande Historical Collections/Clyde W. Tombaugh Papers, Ms407: 15, 34; North Wind Picture Archives: 25; Photo Researchers, NY: 36 (Dr. Juerg Alean/SPL), 57, 102 (Simon Fraser/SPL), 85 (Dennis Milon/SPL), 42, 50, 92, 98 (Space Telescope Science Institute/NASA/SPL), 10, 82, 83, 97 (SPL); Photri Inc.: 27, 67, 73, 108; The Image Bank/Getty Images: 22; United States Naval Observatory: 46.

The photograph on the cover shows an illustration of Pluto. The photograph opposite the title page shows artwork of Pluto and Charon.

Library of Congress Cataloging-in-Publication Data
    Tocci, Salvatore.
    A look at Pluto / by Salvatore Tocci.
    p. cm. – (Out of this world)
Summary: Describes the discovery and observation of the ninth planet, Pluto, and what has been learned about its orbit, its makeup, and its moon.
Includes bibliographical references and index.
    ISBN 0-531-12245-X (lib. bdg.) 0-531-15569-2 (pbk.)
    1. Pluto (Planet)—Juvenile literature. [1. Pluto (Planet).] I. Title. II. Out of this world (Franklin Watts, Inc.)
QB701 .T63 2003   2002002022

FRANKLIN WATTS and associated logos are trademarks and or registered trademarks of Grolier Publishing Co., Inc. SCHOLASTIC and associated logos are trademarks and or registered trademarks of Scholastic Inc.

2 3 4 5 6 7 8 9 10 R 12 11 10 09 08 07 06 05 04

Acknowledgments

I would like to thank Margaret W. Carruthers, planetary geologist, and Sam Storch, lecturer at the American Museum of Natural History's Hayden Planetarium, whose comments and suggestions were extremely helpful in revising my manuscript so that the content was not only accurate but current. My most sincere appreciation is reserved for Melissa Palestro, whose support and editorial insight have guided me through many projects on which we have worked together.

Contents

A Look at Pluto

The *Hubble Space Telescope (HST)* captured this image of Pluto and its moon, Charon, in 1994.

Chapter 1

Planet X

After searching for more than eight months, Clyde Tombaugh finally found what he had been looking for. The date was February 18, 1930. At that time, scientists knew of eight planets that orbited the Sun. But for years, scientists had suspected that a ninth planet existed. They believed that this ninth planet was in an orbit beyond Neptune, which at that time was the farthest known planet from the Sun. Even though they had never seen it, scientists gave this unknown planet a name—Planet X. That day in 1930, Tombaugh thought he had found Planet X.

Clues that Planet X existed came from observations that *astronomers*, scientists who study space, made of Neptune's orbit.

How Science Works: Gravity

Throw a ball up into the air, and Earth's gravity will cause it to fall back down to the ground. But if gravity is a force of attraction between two objects, then Earth should also be attracted to the ball. In other words, Earth should move toward the ball. In fact, Earth does move toward the ball. However, this distance Earth moves is so extremely small that scientists could never hope to measure it. Why does gravity cause the ball to drop from the air and Earth practically not to move at all? The answer can be found by examining the two factors that determine the gravitational force between two objects, such as a ball and Earth.

The gravitational force between two objects depends on their masses and the distance between them. Mass is the quantity of matter that an object has. The more mass the objects have, the greater the gravitational force between them. The closer the objects are, the greater the gravitational force between them.

In proportion to their mass the gravitational force exerted by Earth on the ball in the air is equal to the gravitational force exerted by the ball on Earth. Although the forces are equal, they act in opposite directions. If the gravitational forces are equal and opposite, then why doesn't Earth move half the distance that separates it from the ball? Because the ball's mass is so much less than Earth's, a small force—a toss—is enough to get it moving away from Earth. Then Earth's stronger gravitational pull brings the ball back.

Astronomers know that the orbit a planet follows as it travels around the Sun is affected by the Sun and all the other planets. The Sun and the planets pull on each other because of *gravity*. Gravity is a force of attraction between two objects. The force of gravity between the Sun and planets attracts them to one another, affecting the shape of their orbits. In studying the planet's orbits, astronomers observed something very unusual about the orbits of Neptune and Uranus.

Uranus, the seventh planet in orbit from the Sun, had been spotted in 1781. As early as the 1840s, astronomers noticed that Uranus did not orbit the Sun as they had predicted. Astronomers soon suspected that one or perhaps even more planets existed, pulling on Uranus and causing its orbit to differ from what they had expected. In 1846, Neptune was discovered. But like Uranus, Neptune was found to travel in an orbit that differed from what astronomers had expected. Yet still another unknown planet—a ninth planet—must be out there, this one pulling on Neptune.

Tombaugh was not the first astronomer to look for this ninth planet. In 1877, David Todd had closely searched the skies with his telescope for this ninth planet. Every clear, moonless night for four months, Todd examined some three thousand tiny points of light in the sky. They all turned out to be stars. Todd knew this because the position of each of these points of light in the sky did not change when he observed them several nights apart.

When searching for a new planet, astronomers measure the *parallax* of the object in space. Parallax is the apparent movement of an object when it is viewed from two different positions. To understand what parallax is, hold one finger vertically, close to your face and between your eyes. Turn to face a blank wall. Close your right eye while keeping your left eye open. Then close your left eye and open your right eye. Obviously, you are not moving your finger, but your finger seems to move from one side to the other as you keep opening and closing each eye.

Now hold your finger at arm's length from your face. Again, keep one eye open while closing the other one. Your finger still seems to jump from side to side, but not as much. The farther away the object is, the smaller the jump. If the object is very far away, it will not seem to jump or move at all.

So Far Away

Stars are very far away from Earth. The nearest star is the Sun, which is 93 million miles (150 million kilometers) from Earth. The next nearest star, named Proxima Centauri, is about three hundred thousand times farther away than the Sun. This star is 25 trillion miles (40 trillion km) from Earth! Other stars are even farther away. Planets in our solar system are much closer to Earth than the stars, except for our Sun.

Every day, Earth travels about 1.6 million miles (2.6 million km) along its orbit around the Sun. In just six days, Earth travels about 10 million miles (16 million km) in space. Looking at the sky six nights apart is like having two sets of eyes 10 million miles (16 million km) apart from each other. An object, like a star, that is so very far away will not seem to move at all in the sky over the course of those six nights. But something much closer to Earth, like a planet, will appear to move through the night sky. This is exactly what Clyde Tombaugh saw in 1930 when he looked closely at two photographs that he had taken through his telescope six nights apart.

In his eight-month search for Planet X, Tombaugh had closely examined hundreds of photographs he had taken through his telescope. In all, he had photographed about ninety million stars. Looking at all these images of stars in hopes of finding Planet X obviously took considerable patience and care. The first photograph that revealed Planet X had been taken on January 23, 1930. The next photograph showing the planet had been taken six days later, on January 29. In effect, Tombaugh had two sets of eyes 10 million miles (16 million km) apart from each other looking at the same spot in the night sky.

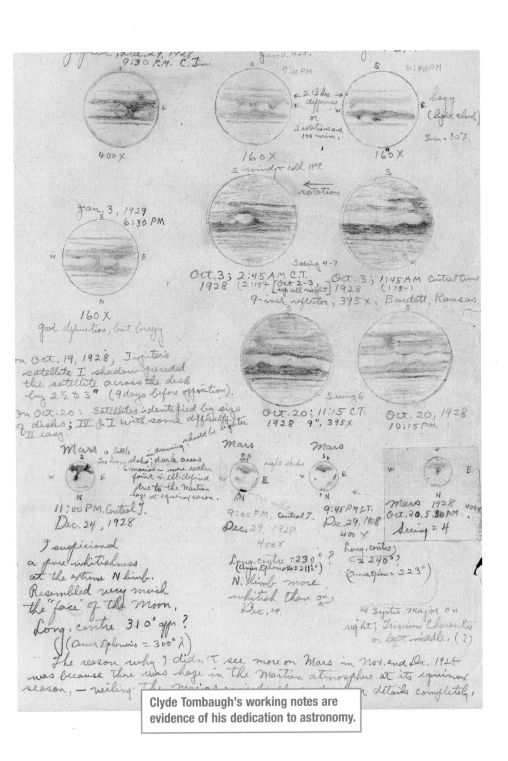

Clyde Tombaugh's working notes are evidence of his dedication to astronomy.

Pluto, which is marked by arrows, moves among the fixed star patterns in the sky.

Hidden among the vast number of images Tombaugh spotted was one that had seemed to move over those six nights. He was thrilled, but he had to be absolutely sure before he told anyone. For the next hour or so, he carefully measured distances between the images on the two photographs. In comparing the two photographs, he discovered that one of the hundreds of light spots had moved about one-eighth of an inch (3 millimeters). Tombaugh quickly informed one of his fellow astronomers that he had found Planet X. Telling the world would be another matter.

A Moving Point of Light

Before announcing a discovery, scientists must be absolutely sure of their findings. If their work involves experiments, scientists will repeat them many times. Only if the experiments produce the same results will they make an announcement of their discovery. In Tombaugh's case, he had to take more photographs. Only when these photographs confirmed that a point of light had moved in the night sky could Tombaugh announce to the world that he had found Planet X. It was not until February 18 that Tombaugh found the time to examine the photographs that he had taken on January 23 and 29. That February night he was anxious to take more photographs, but the day had been cloudy and snowy. He waited to see if the evening sky would start to clear. It didn't.

Unable to work, Tombaugh went to the movies. When he walked outside, it was still cloudy. He waited anxiously until 2 a.m., but the sky never cleared. There was nothing he could do except go to bed. When Tombaugh awoke the next morning, the sky was clear. That night he started taking more photographs. He would take many more photographs over the next several weeks. These photographs confirmed what he had seen earlier: a point of light had moved in the night sky over the course of several nights.

Finally, on the evening of March 12, 1930, Tombaugh and his fellow astronomers were ready to announce the discovery of Planet X. They scheduled their announcement for the next day, March 13, the same date on which Uranus had been discovered 149 years earlier. Tombaugh made the announcement from the Lowell Observatory in Flagstaff, Arizona.

The observatory had been named after Percival Lowell, another astronomer who had searched for Planet X. Lowell died in 1916, obviously having failed in his search. But Planet X turned out to be very near the place in the sky where Lowell had predicted it would be. The news from the Lowell Observatory spread quickly throughout the country. Reporters sought interviews with Tombaugh. Visitors poured in to see the place where the ninth planet had been discovered. Fellow astronomers from all over the country came to see Tombaugh's photographs firsthand. Many were amazed at what he had accomplished.

Most of these astronomers had no idea of what Tombaugh had to go through until they saw the photographs. Some astronomers could barely see some of the images because they were so faint. They also wondered how Tombaugh's eyes could stand peering day after day through the instrument that he used to measure distances between the images on the photographs. Tombaugh explained that he adjusted the instrument so that his eyes were under no more strain than that caused by looking out a window. But he did admit that concentrating on what he was looking at was a problem. Every twenty minutes, he took a short break. After an hour of work, he rested his eyes for thirty minutes.

Percival Lowell

Percival Lowell, who lived from 1855 until 1916, read a report on Mars when he was twenty-two. From that point in his life, Lowell focused his interest on astronomy. Because his family was wealthy, he had no financial obstacles in pursuing his interest. In 1894, Lowell even built his own observatory in Arizona, where the night skies were usually clear, for astronomers to make their observations. For the next fifteen years, Lowell used a 24-inch (61-centimeter) telescope to study Mars.

His drawings of Mars showed hundreds of lines that crossed at various points on the planet. Lowell believed that these lines were canals. He called the points where the canals crossed oases, believing that they were patches of vegetation. In contrast to these oases, which appeared dark through his telescope, Lowell claimed the bright areas he saw on Mars were deserts. Lowell claimed that water melted from Mars's polar ice cap and flowed through the canals to nourish the vegetation. He also believed that the canals on Mars had been built by intelligent beings who once lived on the planet. His views on Mars were published in three books between 1895 and 1908. The suggestion that Mars had canals was definitely dispelled in the 1960s when spacecraft flying by the planet provided clear images of its surface.

During the last eight years of his life, Lowell switched his interest from Mars to finding Planet X. In 1915, he published a paper stating where he believed the planet existed in the solar system. In looking at photographs taken that year at the Lowell Observatory, scientists spotted two faint images of Pluto. However, scientists did not notice these images until after Tombaugh's discovery of Pluto in 1930.

Percival Lowell looks through a 24-inch telescope at the Lowell Observatory in Flagstaff, Arizona.

The point of light from Planet X that showed up on Tombaugh's photographs was very faint. Scientists had expected that the light coming from Planet X would be dim. One reason is that the planet was farther out than Neptune. Also, astronomers expected that Planet X would be small. As a result, they calculated that Planet X would turn out to be 10 to 20 times fainter than Neptune. Actually, Planet X turned out to be 250 times fainter than Neptune.

Naming Planet X

Once Tombaugh and his fellow astronomers had announced their discovery, their next job was to give Planet X a name. Tombaugh received suggestions from all over the country and the world. Lowell's widow even suggested some names. First she proposed that the new planet be named Zeus. This would follow the custom of naming the planets after figures in Greek and Roman mythology. Zeus was the Greek god who was the ruler of the heavens and the father of the other gods. But Lowell's widow soon changed her mind. Instead of Zeus, she wanted the planet named after her late husband, Percival. Twice more she changed her mind, next suggesting Lowell and then finally her own given name, Constance. These suggestions were ignored. No astronomer wanted to break tradition by naming a planet after a person.

Tombaugh favored the name Minerva, who was the Roman goddess of wisdom. However, that name had already been given to one of the *asteroids*. An asteroid is a big rock left over from the formation of our solar system some 4.6 billion years ago. Most asteroids orbit the Sun in a belt between Mars and Jupiter. Unable to use the name Minerva, Tombaugh came across a suggestion sent to him by an eleven-year-old girl living in England. She suggested that Planet X be named

In Greek mythology, Pluto was the lord of the underworld. With his brothers Zeus and Poseidon (called Jupiter and Neptune by the Romans), he ruled the world.

after the Greek god of the underworld. This god was also the brother of Jupiter and Neptune and a son of Saturn, names from Roman mythology that had been used for three of the planets. Tombaugh thought the girl's suggestion was perfect. So Planet X was named Pluto.

In this digitally created image of Pluto, its dark appearance suggests why it might be associated with a mythological god of the underworld.

Chapter 2

An Unusual Orbit

Pluto was the most appropriate name for Tombaugh's newly discovered planet. As god of the underworld, Pluto could make himself invisible. Because it is so far from the Sun, the planet Pluto is so dimly lit that it is invisible to our eyes, even on a clear night. The only way to see the planet is through a telescope that can gather enough light to detect a very dim object, such as Pluto, in the night sky. You would then have to pick it out from among the twenty-million-plus stars you would also see with the telescope. This is far more than the three thousand stars you can see with your eyes on a clear night.

Soon after the announcement of Pluto's discovery on March 13, the Lowell Observatory began receiving urgent requests from many astronomers. With so many stars visible through a telescope, astronomers wanted to know exactly where to look for Pluto in the night sky. Now that Pluto had been discovered, every astronomer wanted to be the first to describe its orbit. Of course, the astronomers at the Lowell Observatory, including Tombaugh, wanted to do the same.

To calculate a planet's orbit, astronomers use mathematical laws that were developed by Johannes Kepler in the early 1600s. At that time, six planets were known—Mercury, Venus, Earth, Mars, Jupiter, and Saturn. Some sixty years earlier, a Polish astronomer named Nicolaus Copernicus had published a book titled *On the Revolution of the Heavenly Spheres*. In his book, Copernicus rejected the commonly accepted belief that the Sun and other planets traveled in orbits around Earth. Instead, Copernicus wrote that all the planets, including Earth, orbit the Sun. He said that their orbits were perfect circles as they traveled around the Sun.

Based on his observations of the planets about sixty years later, Kepler disagreed with Copernicus's statement that the planets orbited the Sun in perfect circles. Kepler reasoned that each planet orbits the Sun in an *ellipse*. An ellipse is a circle that is elongated or stretched out so that it is somewhat flattened. The shape of a planet's orbit is described by Kepler's first law: the orbit of a planet around the Sun is an ellipse. Soon after followed Kepler's second law: a planet moves more rapidly when it is closer to the Sun and more slowly when it is farther from the Sun. The last was Kepler's third law, which used a simple equation to calculate the length of a planet's "year," or the time it took to complete one revolution around the Sun.

In the 1600s, Kepler's three laws became the basis for calculating the orbits of the six planets known at that time. Today, with the help of technology, including instruments that travel deep into space and

The Polish astronomer Nicolaus Copernicus is generally credited with proposing that Earth and the other planets were part of a solar system, in which they revolved around the sun.

Copernicus's book, *On the Revolution of the Heavenly Spheres*, was published in 1543. That year is considered by many scientists to be the start of the scientific revolution. Prior to the publication of Copernicus's book, the description of how nature operated was based mainly on intuition, reasoning, and debate rather than on observation, experimentation, and calculation. As a result, early astronomers were often confused by what they could observe of the planets. For example, the positions of the planets in the night sky were far from where they should have been if they were truly orbiting Earth.

As early as 1507, Copernicus realized that the positions of the planets were exactly where they should be if they all orbited the Sun. By 1530, Copernicus had completed enough observations and cal-culations to conclude that all the planets, including Earth, orbited the Sun. He pre-pared a short summary of his work and sent it to scholars throughout Europe. Most were interested and enthused about his conclusion. However, the events that followed prevented Copernicus from sharing his conclusion with the rest of the world. For one thing, his findings went against the religious and philosophical beliefs that were widely accepted.

Copernicus died from a stroke on May 24, 1543, the same year his book was finally published. Some historians have suggested that Copernicus saw the first copy of his book just before he died. Although some people were convinced that Copernicus was correct, it wasn't until Kepler's work that people generally accepted that the Sun was the center of our solar system.

computers that do millions of calculations per second, astronomers have studied the orbits of these six planets. They found that Kepler was almost but not quite exact in his calculations. Kepler's laws are still used today, almost four hundred years after they were first proposed.

Pluto's Orbit

In 1930, Tombaugh and the other astronomers at the Lowell Observatory were among the first to use Kepler's laws to study Pluto's orbit. But up to this point, the work of the Lowell Observatory astronomers

This illustration shows Pluto's position in the solar system in relation to other planets.

did not involve calculating orbits. Many years had passed since any of them had taken a course using Kepler's laws. To calculate Pluto's orbit, the astronomers at the Lowell Observatory needed help. So they brought in an astronomer who, years earlier, had taught them how to use Kepler's laws to calculate orbits.

Two weeks after the discovery of Pluto had been announced, Tombaugh and his fellow astronomers began working furiously on calculating its orbit. In the meantime, they ignored requests from others for details on Pluto's position. On April 12, 1930, the astronomers at the Lowell Observatory had calculated its orbit. They were shocked by their results. They discovered that Pluto had a very strange orbit. To get a better idea of its orbit, they made a three-dimensional model. What they saw confused them. They immediately announced their findings to the world.

The response from other astronomers was quick. Several of them suggested that because of its strange orbit, Pluto was a *comet* and not a planet. A comet is a ball of rock and ice that travels around the Sun from the outer edge of the solar system. Comets follow long orbits that are shaped much like the one Pluto seemed to follow. The suggestion that Pluto was a comet was based not only on its unusual orbit but also on its small size. The Lowell Observatory astronomers had calculated that Pluto was about the same size as Mars, which is much bigger than any known comet. In addition, no one had ever observed a comet while it was as far out as Saturn. Pluto was far deeper than that into space.

After they had announced their description of Pluto's orbit, the Lowell Observatory astronomers gave others its exact position in the sky. Soon astronomers all over the world were busy photographing and studying this new planet. Some even began to look more closely at photographs that they had taken before 1930. To their surprise, they too saw Pluto. In fact, images of Pluto were found on four photographs taken by an astronomer in 1914. If this astronomer had looked as carefully and closely as Tombaugh had, he may have discovered Pluto before 1930.

With so many eyes focused on Pluto, its unusual orbit was confirmed by several groups of astronomers. Within a year of being discovered, Pluto's orbit was established and confirmed. Like all the other planets, Pluto obeys Kepler's first law. Pluto's orbit is an ellipse. But there is something very unusual about Pluto's orbit. Pluto is one of the five planets that make up what is known as the *outer solar system.* The other four planets are Jupiter, Saturn, Uranus, and Neptune. Although ellipses, the orbits of these four planets are rather close to being true circles. The orbits of these four planets range from 1 percent to 5 percent from being true circles. In contrast, Pluto's orbit is 25 percent from being a true circle. This is even greater than that of any of the planets that make up the *inner solar system,* which are Mercury, Venus, Earth, and Mars. Because the orbits of the inner planets are closer to the Sun, their shapes are expected to be less like a circle and more like an ellipse. But even the orbit of Mercury, the planet closest to the Sun, is only 21 percent from being a true circle. So among all the planets, Pluto still holds the record for having an orbit that is most like an ellipse and least like a circle.

Most of the time, Pluto is the farthest planet from the Sun. Pluto also has the greatest distance to travel to make one complete revolution around the Sun. Being closer, Earth takes only 365 ¼ days, or one Earth year, to orbit the Sun. In contrast, Pluto takes 248 Earth years to complete its orbit around the Sun. Pluto had made only one revolution around the Sun between 1682, when Halley's Comet was seen streaking across the night sky, and 1930, when Tombaugh discovered Pluto.

Because their orbits are ellipses, all the planets are closer to the Sun at some times than at others. But because its orbit is most like an ellipse, Pluto's distance from the Sun varies the most. The closest Pluto comes to the Sun is 2.8 billion miles (4.5 billion km). Even at its closest point, Pluto is still thirty times farther from the Sun than Earth.

The farthest Pluto gets from the Sun is 4.6 billion miles (7.4 billion km). This is almost fifty times greater than the distance between Earth and the Sun. At this distance, the Sun as seen from Pluto would look like a tiny white dot in the sky.

Changing Places

The elliptical shape of Pluto's orbit also results in something that no other planet does. At times, Pluto's orbit crosses Neptune's orbit. When this happens, Neptune becomes the ninth and farthest planet from the Sun. Pluto then becomes the eighth planet in the solar system. This reversal occurs for 20 out of every 248 Earth years that it takes Pluto to orbit the Sun. The last time Pluto's orbit took it inside that of Neptune's occurred between January 1979 and February 1999. Pluto will remain the farthest planet in orbit from the Sun until September 2226, when Neptune will once again take its place.

When astronomers first discovered that Pluto and Neptune exchanged places, they wondered if the two planets might crash into each other at some point. But another strange thing about Pluto's orbit prevents this from ever happening. Pluto's orbit is tilted. For the most part, the orbits of all the other planets are oriented at an angle close to one another.

To understand what this means, hold your right hand flat in front of your eyes. Point your thumb slightly downward. Keep your other four fingers together and flat. Notice that these four fingers are aligned at the same angle. These fingers represent the orbits of eight planets, with the exception of Pluto's. The orbits of these eight planets are aligned within a few degrees of one another, just like your fingers.

Now look at your thumb. Your thumb represents the angle of Pluto's orbit. Notice that it is tilted compared to the others. Pluto's orbit is actually tilted about 17 degrees from that of most of the other planets. Pluto and Neptune will never collide mainly for two reasons. First, their orbits are not aligned at the same angle. This means that Pluto orbits the Sun at a point in space that is sometimes "above" Neptune's orbit and at other times "below" it. Second, for every three orbits that Neptune makes around the Sun, Pluto makes only two orbits. As a result, Neptune and Pluto will never crash into each other. In fact, the closest the two planets come to each other is 1.3 billion miles (2 billion km).

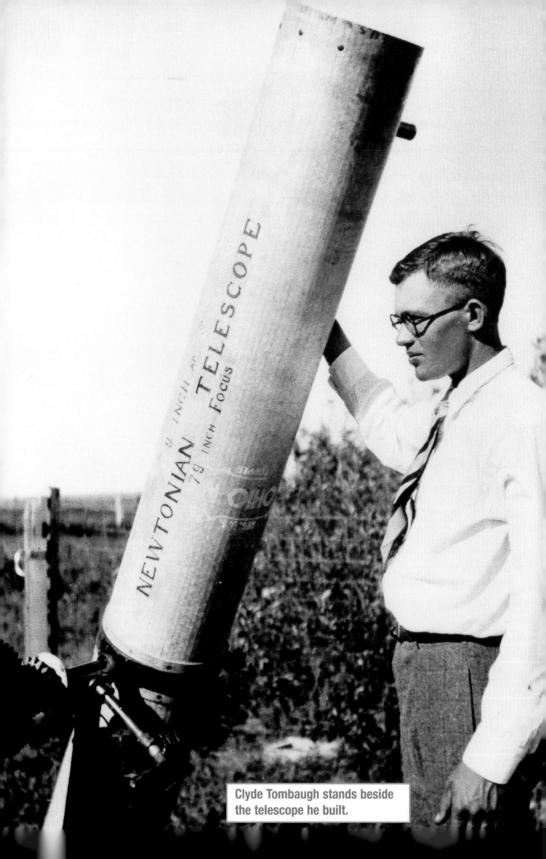

Clyde Tombaugh stands beside the telescope he built.

Chapter 3

So Far Away

As a sixth-grader growing up on a farm in Illinois in the late 1910s, Clyde Tombaugh had wondered what the geography on other planets was like. His uncle, who lived on a nearby farm, would help him search for the answers. Tombaugh's uncle was an amateur astronomer who would often look at the night sky with his simple telescope. Whenever the family got together on weekends, his uncle would let Tombaugh look through the telescope. He even let Tombaugh take the telescope home for several weeks at a time.

The telescope had a 3-inch (7.5-cm) lens to magnify objects. In other words, the *diameter* of the lens in this telescope measured 3 inches (7.5 cm). Peering through this telescope, Tombaugh could see

Tombaugh's decision to become an astronomer was based in part on an incident that occurred on his family farm on June 20, 1928. That day, a terrible hailstorm struck. With only about a fifteen-minute warning, all his family could do was to get the horses and cows into the barn. The heavy rains destroyed the 20 acres (8 hectares) of oats that were just about ready to be harvested. The stalks had been beaten into the ground, where they were covered with mud. The Tombaughs realized that they would not have a crop to sell and would be broke until the following year. Clyde decided that day that farming was not for him. The first chance he had, he was going to leave home and search for a job. He thought of two possibilities. One was to set up a small business to sell telescopes that he would make. The other was to apply for a job on the railroad with the hope of someday becoming an engineer.

During the fall of 1928, Tombaugh started making drawings of what he observed through his 13-inch (33-cm) telescope of Jupiter and Mars. He sent several of his drawings to the Lowell Observatory, which he had read about in some old copies of a magazine called *Popular Astronomy*. Almost immediately, Tombaugh received a response. After exchanging letters, he was asked if he would be interested in coming to work at the Lowell Observatory on a trial basis for a few months. The staff at the observatory was about to put a new telescope into operation and could use his help. He was warned that the telescope would be housed in an unheated building where the temperature could get quite cold during the night. Without any hesitation, Tombaugh accepted the invitation and left for the Lowell Observatory on January 14, 1929. He did not even have enough money in his pocket for a return ticket should things not work out.

Tombaugh's astronomical observations were good enough to win him a spot at the Lowell Observatory

the craters on our Moon, the rings of Saturn, the moons of Jupiter, and the phases of Venus. But no matter how hard he looked, Tombaugh would never have been able to find Pluto with this telescope. It wasn't even close to being able to gather enough light to see that far into space.

To find Pluto in 1930, Tombaugh used a 13-inch (33-cm) telescope. In addition, a camera was attached to the telescope. The combination of the telescope and the camera could probe a large area of the night sky. More important, it could look deep into space where Pluto lies hidden in the dark.

For forty years following Pluto's discovery, scientists struggled to learn more about Pluto. They faced several obstacles. First, Pluto is very far from Earth, on average some 3 billion miles (4.8 billion km) away. Trying to study Pluto with a telescope is like trying to study something as small as a walnut 30 miles (48 km) away. Second, these scientists did not have the technology that is available today to study objects so far away in space. Despite these obstacles, the scientists still tried to learn more about Pluto other than merely its location in space and the nature of its orbit. For one thing, they wanted to know its mass.

To calculate Pluto's mass, Tombaugh used what other astronomers had discovered about Pluto. Shortly after Pluto's discovery in March 1930, astronomers had pointed a 100-inch (254-cm) telescope at the planet. At that time, this was the largest and most powerful telescope in the world. Even with this telescope, astronomers were aware that they would not be able to see any details on Pluto's surface. What they could do, however, was use this powerful telescope to get a closer look at the light coming from Pluto. They discovered that Pluto's light was

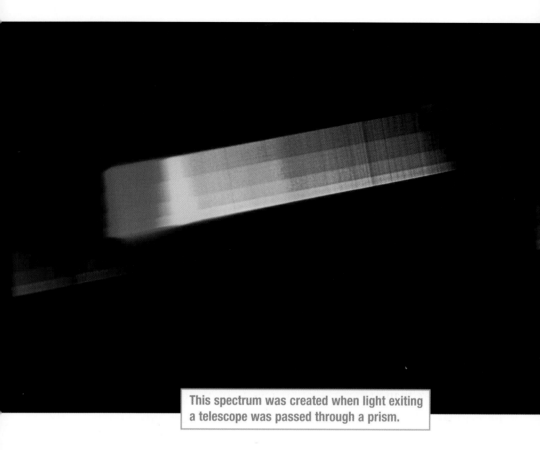

This spectrum was created when light exiting a telescope was passed through a prism.

very much like the Sun's light. In the 1930s, astronomers knew much about the Sun's light.

The light coming from the Sun or a planet can be examined with an instrument called a *spectrograph*. A spectrograph separates the light into different wavelengths. Each wavelength represents a different color. All matter is made from chemical *elements*, such as oxygen, carbon, and iron. Each element gives off specific wavelengths of light when it is heated. By examining the wavelengths that are given off, scientists can determine which elements are present. Knowing the elements that are present helps scientists determine the mass of an object.

Pluto's Mass

While he was searching for Planet X, Tombaugh suspected that it would turn out to have a very large mass. He reasoned that only such a large mass could account for both Neptune and Uranus moving along an unexpected path around the Sun. But Tombaugh's calculations came up with a much smaller mass for Pluto than he expected to find.

Tombaugh calculated that Pluto had a mass three times greater than Earth's. But he had also calculated that the planet should have a mass about seven times greater than Earth's to account for Neptune's and Uranus's orbits. This led Tombaugh to believe that there might be even more planets deep in space, traveling in orbits beyond that of Pluto and affecting the orbits of Neptune and Uranus. Perhaps the real Planet X still remained to be found. Over the next fourteen years, Tombaugh searched hard for another planet. During that time, he examined more than ninety million images on photographs he took of the night sky. Despite his heroic efforts, Tombaugh never discovered another planet.

In his search for another planet, Tombaugh used telescopes that were more powerful than the one he had used to discover Pluto. Even though telescopes were becoming more and more powerful, it would take until the 1990s before anyone got a better look at Pluto. The problem came from the fact that all light coming from outer space must pass through Earth's atmosphere. Earth's atmosphere causes images photographed through a telescope to appear blurred. When a person looks through a telescope at distant planets, the images appear fuzzy because Earth's atmosphere scatters the light coming from the Sun.

All planets appear as tiny points of light in the night sky because of the sunlight that reflects off their surfaces. The closer a planet is to Earth, the brighter it appears and the easier it is for scientists to pick out various details. For example, scientists can see blurry patches on Mars, dense clouds covering Venus, and colored bands circling Jupiter.

But with Pluto being so far away, its light is very dim by the time it reaches Earth. At its brightest, Pluto is still one million times dimmer than Jupiter, the planet in the outer solar system that is closest to Earth. Thus, for some sixty years after its discovery, scientists could not see a single detail on Pluto's surface. Fortunately, they had other methods to get information about this distant planet not long after its discovery. In fact, one of these methods was used by an astronomer during the same month in 1930 in which Pluto had been discovered.

Studying the Light from Pluto

The astronomer passed the sunlight reflecting off Pluto through different-colored filters. Sunlight is actually a mixture of all the colors of the rainbow—red, orange, yellow, green, blue, indigo, and violet. If all these colors are present in the proper proportions, then the light will be a true white. However, if one of the colors, like red, is present in a higher proportion, then the white light will have a reddish tinge. But Pluto was too far away for astronomers to detect any tinge in its white color with just their eyes. Here is where the colored filters became helpful.

In 1930, the astronomer Carl Lampland photographed the light coming from Pluto after it passed through a yellow filter. He also passed Pluto's light through a blue filter. Lampland found that the light was brighter after it passed through the yellow filter. This meant that Pluto's light had more yellow in it than scientists had thought. This yellow light could pass through the yellow filter but not the blue filter. Therefore, the light passing through the yellow filter was brighter. In contrast, Lampland found that the light coming from Neptune had more blue in it than scientists had thought. By 1933, astronomers had gathered enough evidence to say that Pluto was a yellowish planet, while Neptune was a bluish planet.

Unfortunately, knowing that Pluto reflected a yellowish color did not tell astronomers very much. This did not give them much of a clue as to what the surface or atmosphere of Pluto is like. Then why did they bother going through the trouble of carrying out this experiment? The simple answer is that in the 1930s that was about all they could do to study a planet that is so far away. For some twenty years after Pluto's discovery, the only information known about the planet was its orbit, its mass, and that it reflected a yellowish light. Starting in the 1950s, technology began providing scientists with the tools they needed to learn more about Pluto. One of these tools is called a *photomultiplier tube*, or PMT for short.

Like the photographic film that Tombaugh used, a PMT can detect a light spot. But a PMT is more powerful than film. As its name suggests, a PMT multiplies or amplifies a light signal it receives, like a microphone amplifies a sound signal that it receives. Therefore, a PMT is much more sensitive to light. Armed with a PMT, a scientist could learn more about Pluto's light. In 1954, this is exactly what they set about doing. What they found surprised them.

Pluto's Rotation and Atmosphere

Scientists discovered that the light coming from Pluto changed over a period of time more than that of the other planets except Mars. What really surprised them was that there was a pattern to this change. They observed that the pattern repeated itself every 6.39 Earth days, or every 6 days, 9 hours, and 21½ minutes, plus or minus 4½ minutes. Scientists knew that Earth takes 24 hours, or 1 Earth day, to rotate once on its axis. They concluded that Pluto takes 6.39 Earth days, or about 153 hours, to do the same. This was remarkable because up to that point they knew that no planet beyond Earth took more than 25 hours to rotate. They wondered why Pluto rotates so slowly.

The PMTs also revealed information about Pluto's atmosphere, or, perhaps, its lack of an atmosphere. The changes in light the PMTs detected formed a pattern that was repeated every 6.39 days. It was like listening to a song that lasts for 6.39 days. As a song plays, there are changes in pitch, volume, and harmony. But once it finishes, the song starts all over and plays exactly as it had before. This is the way the light from Pluto acted. There would be changes in Pluto's light during the 6.39 days, but then it would pass through exactly the same changes at the same times all over again.

From this information, scientists concluded that Pluto had little, if any, atmosphere. If it did, then the atmosphere would have to be a cloud-free one. To understand how they arrived at their conclusion, imagine that you are shining a flashlight on a wall in a dark room. If you kept waving your hand in front of the flashlight, the pattern of light rays that you would see on the wall would keep changing.

Like a moving hand in front of a flashlight, clouds constantly move across the sky. What's more, they keep changing their shapes.

Any clouds over Pluto would then constantly change how sunlight bounces off the surface of the planet and travels to Earth. Thus, any clouds around Pluto affect the light that the PMTs detect. As a result, the scientists would not see the same exact pattern of light changes repeated every 6.39 days.

In the 1950s, scientists knew that each planet of the outer solar system had an atmosphere with thick clouds and that each rotated on its axis much faster than Pluto. Pluto was proving to be a very different kind of outer planet. In 1978, scientists would discover just how different Pluto is.

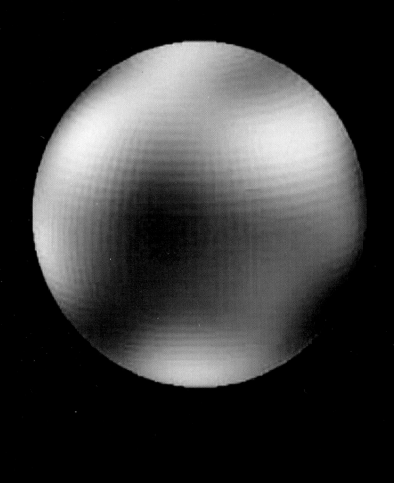

This is a computer-generated image of Pluto created from observations made by the *HST*. The image is designed to emphasize Pluto's various bright and dark regions.

Chapter 4

Another Discovery

ircling the Sun in its unusual orbit, Pluto was some 800 million miles (1.3 billion km) closer to Earth in 1978 than it had been in 1930. Being that much closer, Pluto appeared twice as bright to anyone looking at it from Earth. With the help of telescopes much more powerful than the one that Tombaugh had used to discover Pluto, scientists could get much better photographs of the planet. One such group was working at the United States Naval Observatory in Washington, D.C. Among them was an astronomer named James Christy.

On the night of June 22, 1978, Christy was working at the observatory. It was a Thursday night. That weekend he and his family were going to move from their apartment to a new home they had just purchased. The whole family had been busy packing for the move. As a result, Christy did not have the time to spend on a major project at the observatory. He had kept busy by undertaking smaller tasks that he knew he could finish before his move. Among those tasks was one that his boss gave him to do that Thursday night.

Christy was asked to measure some distances on photographs that had recently been taken of Pluto. One thing scientists hoped to accomplish while Pluto was so much closer to Earth was to get a more accurate picture of its orbit. In all, there were eighteen images of Pluto to be measured. But Christy was told that some of the photographs were marked "defective." The photographs had been taken at the naval observatory in Flagstaff, only several miles from the Lowell Observatory where Tombaugh had discovered Pluto. Rather than ignore these "defective" images, Christy decided to take a look at them for himself. He soon noticed that there was something very unusual about them.

Pluto's shape appeared slightly elongated, as if it had been stretched out or bulged in one spot. Those who first saw these images felt that perhaps Earth's atmosphere had caused Pluto's light to be more blurred than usual. Or perhaps the telescope had not properly tracked Pluto as it moved in its orbit. But then Christy noticed something else on the photographs. All the stars looked perfectly round. If Earth's atmosphere were responsible, then all the images on the photographs should have a bulge, not just Pluto. Christy immediately realized that the images of Pluto were not defective. They were showing scientists that there was something new to be learned about Pluto.

Examining the Possibilities

Photographs taken in April 1978 showed that Pluto's image had a slight bulge pointing south. Photos taken in May showed that Pluto had a slight bulge pointing north. At first, Christy thought that he had discovered a giant mountain range on Pluto. But he quickly realized that no mountain range could be so tall as to produce the images he was looking at. Christy next thought that these images revealed that a giant volcano was erupting on Pluto. But he knew that a volcano was highly unlikely to erupt that dramatically for as long as a month.

Then another thought struck Christy. He kept thinking about the length of time that had passed between the two photographs—a month. What, if anything, did this mean? His thoughts wandered to Earth. What changes occur over a period of a month on Earth? He then realized what these photographs revealed: Pluto must have a moon, just like Earth.

Like Tombaugh, Christy had to verify his discovery. So he asked Robert Harrington, another astronomer at the observatory, to look at the photographs. Both agreed that examining the images of Pluto was far from easy. Even though Pluto was now much closer to Earth and twice as bright, it still formed a very small image that measured only about ¼ inch (6 mm) on a photograph. The bulge measured less than half that! Harrington suggested that the bulge might be caused by a star in the same region of the sky as Pluto. Christy checked a sky atlas and found that no bright stars were in the same region of the sky as Pluto at that time. He finally decided to tell his boss. After all, he was the one who had asked Christy to measure Pluto's images in the first place. When Christy said that he had found a moon orbiting Pluto, his

James Christy (seated) discovered Charon in 1978. Next to him is Robert Harrington, who verified the discovery.

Although Christy is usually recognized as the discoverer of Pluto's moon, Harrington is often mentioned as its codiscoverer. In 1988, ten years after the discovery of Pluto's moon had been announced, Harrington published a paper called "The Location of Planet X." Harrington thought that a tenth planet, which he called Planet X, existed in our solar system. The "X" in the planet's name was based on the Roman numeral for ten. In his paper, Harrington wrote that Pluto and its moon could not be responsible for both Uranus and Neptune following unexpected paths in their orbits around the Sun. He reasoned that there still must be at least one more planet waiting to be discovered.

In 1990, Harrington reported at a meeting of the American Astronomical Society that he had narrowed his search for Planet X to the southern skies. He also indicated that he was planning to lead a team of scientists to search for this new planet from an observatory in New Zealand. However, Harrington died in 1993 without ever having assembled a team to search for Planet X.

boss told him that it was impossible. Someone would have surely spotted it by now.

The next day, Christy decided to check some photographs of Pluto that the observatory had in its files. These had been taken periodically ever since Pluto had been discovered, almost fifty years earlier. Christy selected some photographs taken in 1970. Checking these carefully, he again found the bulge on the image of Pluto. This time he noticed that the bulge made one complete cycle around Pluto over a period of a week. Christy knew that Pluto made a complete rotation on its axis once every 6.39 days. He thought that something was circling Pluto once every 6.39 days.

Christy immediately proceeded to do some calculating. If this object was circling Pluto once every 6.39 days, then he could figure out where the bulge should appear on the 1978 photographs of the planet based on where it was in the 1970 photographs. But he wanted to be sure that his work would not be biased. Christy hoped that the bulge was something that was circling Pluto, perhaps its moon. However, he did not want this hope to influence what he was about to do. So Christy asked a colleague to do the same calculations. The two of them would not share any information until they had their final answers. When they were both finished, they compared their results. Both had the same answer. What's more, their answer as to where the bulge should be was exactly where it appeared in the 1978 photographs.

Still wanting additional evidence to support his findings, Christy did some more calculations. When he was finished, he checked some photographs of Pluto taken in 1965. Again, the bulge was right where he predicted it should be. Christy next thought it wise to get the closest photographs possible of Pluto. He contacted astronomers at an observatory in Chile. Christy asked if they would photograph Pluto through their 158-inch (4-meter) telescope. These images of Pluto also revealed a bulge on the planet.

The Official Announcement

On July 7, just two weeks after Christy had first examined the 1978 photographs, the U.S. Naval Observatory announced that Pluto had a moon. It had taken Christy less than a day to make his discovery. Astronomers immediately wondered why someone had not seen it sooner. Shortly after Pluto's discovery, astronomers had immediately started looking to see if any *satellites* were orbiting the planet. A satellite is a natural or human-made object that orbits another object, such as a planet, in space. Our Moon is an example of a natural satellite that orbits the Earth. The space shuttle is an example of a human-made satellite that orbits the Earth.

During the same month in which astronomers had announced Pluto's discovery in 1930, the astronomers at the Lowell Observatory, including Tombaugh, started searching for a satellite. Others also tried. Some who tried had taken very good photographs of Pluto. In fact, one astronomer later said that he had observed something strange about Pluto back in 1965. Like Christy, he had noticed the bulge. But unlike Christy, he had thought it was the result of Earth's atmosphere causing Pluto's light to be blurred. What he failed to notice, but what Christy had noticed, was the fact that all the other images in these photographs were round and had no bulges.

Perhaps earlier astronomers had not discovered Pluto's moon because they had faced obstacles that Christy had not. Since 1930, Pluto had been getting closer and closer to Earth. Recall that Pluto was some 800 million miles (1.3 billion km) closer to Earth in 1978 when Christy spotted its moon. Not only was the planet closer and brighter, astronomers had telescopes that could gather much more light than they did in 1930. In the past, astronomers also had to expose their film for a fairly long time in order to capture the dim light coming from Pluto. As a result, their images were not nearly as sharp as those taken in the 1960s and 1970s. Using more sensitive film with shorter exposure times, astronomers started getting much sharper images of Pluto. Only then could its moon possibly be detected. Pluto's moon always stays so close to the planet that only a clear image can reveal its presence. In the past, the images taken with longer exposures made it seem as if the moon was just a part of the planet itself.

Soon after the announcement of its discovery, astronomers had to give Pluto's moon a name. The honor fell to its discoverer, James Christy. It didn't take long for him to come up with a name. He sug-

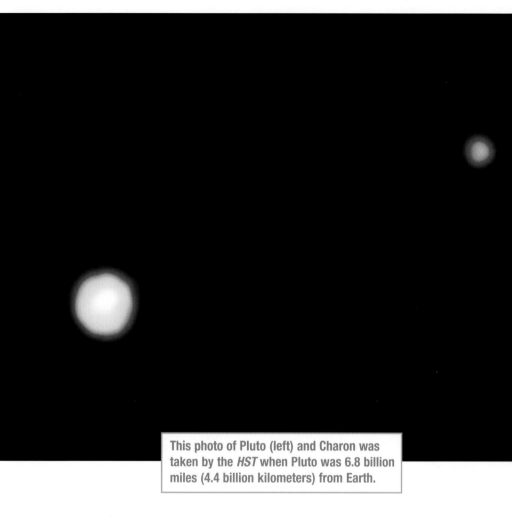

This photo of Pluto (left) and Charon was taken by the *HST* when Pluto was 6.8 billion miles (4.4 billion kilometers) from Earth.

gested naming the moon Charon, based on his wife's name, Charlene. He felt that the name Charon was more scientific-sounding than Charlene. Charon sounded like the proton, neutron, and electron that make up an atom. But Christy soon realized that the rules required that all objects in space be named after someone in Greek or Roman mythology.

A colleague suggested the name Persephone, the wife of Pluto. Christy thought the name was appropriate. While checking a dictionary to get more information about Persephone, something else struck him. He came across the name Charon. He read that Charon was the boatman in Greek mythology who rowed dead souls into Hades, or the underworld, where Pluto reigned as god. Christy had no doubt—Charon was the perfect name for Pluto's moon.

This artist's impression shows
Pluto and its moon, Charon.

Chapter 5

A Double Planet

Charon orbits Pluto at a distance of about 11,800 miles (19,000 km). The only moon that is closer to its planet is Phobos, which orbits Mars. But Charon is much larger than Phobos. Because of Charon's large size and closeness to Pluto, some scientists refer to the two as a double planet.

In 1978, scientists knew that Charon orbits Pluto once every 6.39 days. They also knew that Pluto rotates on its axis once every 6.39 days. That year, a scientist named Leif Anderson discovered something else about the way Pluto and Charon were moving through space. He calculated that they were moving in such a way that each of them would pass in front of the other as seen from Earth. Thus, Charon would block Pluto's view. Then they would exchange places so that

Pluto would block Charon's view. Anderson calculated that two different types of events were involved.

One is a *mutual event*. In astronomy, a mutual event occurs when two objects in space move in such a way as to partially block, or *eclipse,* the view of each other as seen from Earth. A mutual event, then, is a partial eclipse. Anderson calculated that a partial eclipse between Pluto and Charon would periodically occur over a three-year period.

The other type would be a central event. In astronomy, a *central event* occurs when two objects in space move in such a way so that they pass directly in front of one another as seen from Earth. A central event, then, is a total eclipse. Anderson calculated that Pluto would move in such a way as to totally eclipse Charon so that it could not be seen from Earth. In turn, Charon would pass in front of Pluto so that only the outer rim of the planet would be seen from Earth. Anderson calculated that a total eclipse between Pluto and Charon would periodically occur over a two-year period.

Anderson determined that the period of total eclipses would occur both before and after the period of partial eclipses. In all, Pluto and Charon would be passing through eclipses for about seven years. Anderson calculated that these eclipses would take place sometime during the 1970s or 1980s, but he couldn't be sure of the exact time.

Anderson was anxious. It was 1978. These eclipses may have already taken place. If so, it was obviously too late to observe them. If they had taken place, however, surely some astronomer would have noticed them. There was no report of anyone having described these eclipses. For this reason, Anderson concluded that they were going to take place—and soon.

This time-lapse photography sequence shows Pluto and Charon in mutual eclipse.

Astronomers quickly started looking for the eclipses. No one saw any that year. The next year came and went without a single eclipse. The same was true the next year and the year after that. By the end of 1984, not a single eclipse had been observed between Pluto and Charon. Astronomers were beginning to doubt Anderson's prediction. They rechecked his calculations. Sadly, Anderson had died from cancer the year after he had made his prediction. He was only thirty-five.

In reviewing Anderson's calculations, the astronomers could not find any mistakes. They agreed that Pluto and Charon should pass through years of eclipses and that they should start soon. On February 20, 1985, an astronomer observed Pluto passing in front of Charon. The eclipses had begun. They would give astronomers the opportunity to learn much more about this double planet.

Modern Technology

Today, scientists use a digital camera known as a *charged-coupled device*, or CCD for short, to take pictures of objects in space. A CCD translates millions of digits that it detects into an image. The image that a CCD produces would require millions of PMTs like the one used in 1954 to discover the length of Pluto's rotation. Beginning in 1985, CCDs began providing scientists with new and updated information about Pluto and Charon as they passed through their eclipses.

One of the first pieces of information dealt with the sizes of Pluto and Charon. In 1930, Tombaugh discovered just how small Pluto is. Although he could not accurately measure it, he concluded that Pluto was smaller than Mercury, the smallest planet at that time. This meant that Pluto had a diameter less than that of Mercury, or less than some 3,500 miles (5,600 km). After Charon's discovery in 1978, astronomers

How Science Works: Too Close Together

Pluto and Charon are so close together and so far from Earth that scientists have always had problems trying to make separate measurements of the two. However, in 1999, scientists at the Keck Observatory in Hawaii were able to get a good look at Charon. The observatory houses the world's two largest telescopes, known as Keck I and Keck II. Each telescope is eight stories high, weighs 300 tons (272 metric tons), and has a main mirror with a diameter of 394 inches (10 m). Perched atop the Mauna Kea summit, these telescopes can probe the deepest regions of space with little interference from the atmosphere.

By examining the light reflecting off Charon, scientists discovered that the moon is covered with ice crystals that have an unexpected shape. The crystals appear much like those formed when water freezes—neatly ordered and having a hexagonal structure. Scientists were surprised because the frigid temperatures in deep space cause ice crystals to form with a random, broken-down shape that they call amorphous.

The presence of crystalline ice on Charon means that the moon is much warmer than anyone had possibly imagined. Scientists have suggested several possibilities to explain this observation. One possibility is that Charon may have some type of internal heat source. Another possibility is that Charon was hit by a large comet, with heat being released by the impact. A third possibility is that volcanoes were once active on Charon.

Keck I (left) and Keck II are located at the Mauna Kea observatory in Hawaii.

were able to be a little more precise about Pluto's size. But they still could say only that its diameter might be as small as 1,100 miles (1,750 km) or as large as 2,700 miles (4,300 km).

In contrast, astronomers had a better idea of Charon's size. In 1980, an astronomer had calculated it to be almost 750 miles (1,200 km). In 1985, equipped with their CCDs and powerful telescopes, astronomers were set to measure Pluto. They knew the exact speed at which Charon was orbiting Pluto. Simply put, all they had to do was time how long it took for Charon to glide over Pluto, gradually eclipsing the planet's view from Earth.

To get an idea of what they hoped to do, imagine that you are in space looking down on a plane traveling over the United States. As the plane flies across the country, it casts a shadow on the land. Assume the plane is traveling at exactly 500 miles per hour (805 kph). You mark the spot on land where the plane casts its shadow. Exactly two hours later, you mark the spot on land where the plane casts its shadow at that point. To find the distance on land between these two spots, all you would have to do is multiply the plane's speed by the time traveled. In this imaginary case, the distance between the two spots on land would be 500 mph (805 kph) times 2 hours, which equals exactly 1,000 miles (1,610 km).

So all astronomers had to know was how long it took for Charon to cast its shadow over Pluto during a total eclipse. Actually, they had to consider several other factors in their calculations. But at least they had a way to determine Pluto's size more accurately with the help of powerful telescopes, CCDs, and eclipses. The most recent calculations indicate that Pluto's diameter is between 1,430 and 1,450 miles (2,300 and 2,340 km).

Pluto's Size Compared with Earth's

Pluto's diameter is about one-sixth that of Earth. If Earth were the size of a basketball, then Pluto would be the size of a Ping-Pong ball. Pluto is even smaller than Earth's Moon. If Pluto and Charon were placed side by side, they would both fit within the continental United States. Pluto and Charon may be the smallest pair in the solar system, but they do hold a record for large size. Charon is the largest satellite relative to its planet in the solar system. For example, the diameter of our Moon is about one-quarter that of Earth. In contrast, the diameter of Charon is about one-half that of Pluto.

Diameter and Volume

The sizes of planets, such as Pluto and Earth, can be compared in terms of either their diameters or their *volumes*. To compare the sizes of the planets in terms of their diameters, just divide the values of their diameters.

$$\frac{\text{Earth's diameter} = 7,920 \text{ miles}}{\text{Pluto's diameter} = 1,430 \text{ miles}} = 5.54$$

Therefore, Earth's diameter is 5.54 times larger than that of Pluto's. Obviously, this same value would be obtained if you compared their diameters in kilometers.

$$\frac{\text{Earth's diameter} = 12,740 \text{ km}}{\text{Pluto's diameter} = 2,300 \text{ km}} = 5.54$$

However, Earth's volume is many times larger than that of Pluto. Volume is the amount of space an object, like a planet, takes up. The volume of a planet is calculated according to the formula volume = $\frac{4}{3}\pi r^3$, where $\pi = 3.14$ and r = radius or half the diameter.

$$\frac{\text{Earth's volume} = \frac{4}{3}\pi (3,960 \text{ miles})^3}{\text{Pluto's volume} = \frac{4}{3}\pi (715 \text{ miles})^3} =$$

$$\frac{62,100,000,000 \text{ miles}}{365,500,000 \text{ miles}} = 170$$

Therefore, Earth's volume is 170 times larger than that of Pluto's. Notice that the value $\frac{4}{3}\pi$ is in both the numerator and denominator and therefore cancel out each other.

Pluto's Albedo

Now that they had a better measurement of Pluto's size, scientists could learn more about the planet. One of the first things they wanted was a measurement of how bright Pluto is. The brightness of any planet in the night sky is due to the light that it reflects from the Sun. How much of that light a planet reflects partly depends on its size. The larger it is, the more surface the planet has to reflect the light and the brighter it will appear. For its extremely small size, Pluto appears very bright to scientists. In fact, the planet is much brighter than it should be based on its small size.

The brightness of a planet is called its *albedo*. The albedo of an object in space is a measurement of how much of the sunlight that strikes that object is reflected by its surface. For example, the albedo of our Moon is about 12 percent. This means that the Moon reflects about 12 percent of the sunlight that strikes it. Scientists have calculated Pluto's albedo to be about 30 percent. They know that the albedo of most icy objects in space, such as a comet, is about 35 percent. This makes sense, as their bright, icy surfaces reflect more sunlight than the dark, rocky surface of the Moon. But what it also means is that Pluto's surface reflects sunlight as well as freshly fallen snow. Astronomers knew that Pluto's surface could not be covered with snow. It is far too cold. In fact, at that time the average temperature on Pluto was thought to be about −380° F (−230° C). Why, then, is Pluto so bright?

The first part of the answer to this question came from a discovery made in 1976. That year, a team of astronomers used a 158-inch (4-m) telescope to study the light coming from Pluto. They passed this light through a set of five special filters. With the help of these filters, scientists could detect whether the light was reflecting off a surface made of rock or ice. Moreover, scientists could tell if the ice was made of water, ammonia, or methane. For four nights, they studied Pluto very closely. When they were finished, they discovered that Pluto's surface is made of methane ice. Pluto is the only planet cold enough for methane to exist as a solid rather than a gas.

At first, knowing that Pluto's surface is made of methane ice actually created more of a problem in trying to explain why the planet is so bright. In 1979, scientists thought that Pluto most likely did not have any atmosphere and that if it did, the atmosphere was extremely thin. This meant that ultraviolet radiation coming from the Sun could easily strike Pluto's icy surface. This is unlike what happens on Earth, where the ozone layer in our upper atmosphere prevents most of this ultraviolet light from reaching our planet's surface. If all the ultraviolet light did reach Earth, all kinds of medical problems would arise. But on Pluto, there are no living creatures to be affected by all this ultraviolet light. There is, however, all that methane ice on its surface.

Methane reflects light well and so appears very bright. However, ultraviolet light changes methane into other kinds of substances, such as carbon. Carbon, which is basically a dark soot, absorbs light and so appears dark. With all the ultraviolet light striking Pluto, the methane that makes up its icy surface should gradually turn into carbon. Therefore, Pluto should be quite dim. The question as to why Pluto is so bright was becoming more and more difficult to answer.

Proposing a Hypothesis

A possible answer was found by taking another look at Pluto's unusual orbit. In 1988, scientists proposed a *hypothesis* to explain why the planet is so bright. A hypothesis is commonly defined as an educated guess. The emphasis in this definition is on the word "educated." When a scientist proposes a hypothesis, he or she is suggesting an explanation to a question or problem. What is important to realize is that the suggested explanation comes from observations the scientist has collected. In other words, there is a foundation on which a hypothesis is based. In turn, a hypothesis often gives scientists ideas as to how they can proceed to test it.

The hypothesis about Pluto's brightness states that when the planet is closest to the Sun, it is warm enough so that some of the methane ice on the planet's surface melts and then turns into a gas. This gas slowly rises from the surface, giving Pluto a very thin atmosphere made of methane. The materials remaining on its icy surface absorb the sunlight passing through its thin atmosphere, making Pluto darker at this point in its orbit.

As Pluto moves farther and farther from the Sun, the temperature keeps dropping. Soon it gets cold enough for the methane gas in the atmosphere to freeze. This methane ice then falls to Pluto's surface, covering it with a fresh blanket of frost that reflects sunlight. At this point in its orbit, Pluto appears brighter. As Pluto's orbit again takes it toward the Sun, the cycle starts over. Keep in mind that this is a very slow cycle, as it takes Pluto 248 Earth years to complete one orbit around the Sun.

According to these events, Pluto's brightness should vary as it orbits the Sun. In 1987, astronomers found that, in fact, Pluto's light had been brighter in 1950 and had gotten progressively dimmer since then. Since 1950, Pluto was getting closer and closer to the Sun. If the hypothesis is correct, the closer Pluto got to the Sun, the less methane remained in its icy surface. As a result, the surface contained more and more carbon, causing Pluto to get dimmer and dimmer. But this explanation of the change in Pluto's brightness depended on one major assumption—that Pluto has an atmosphere, even if there isn't much of one. Proof that the planet does have an atmosphere came in 1988 when astronomers looked at Pluto in a very different way.

Much of the little that is known about Pluto has been learned in just the last twenty years or so.

Chapter 6

A Clearer Look

The best way to find out if Pluto has an atmosphere would be to observe the planet as it passes in front of, or eclipses, a star. Any light from the star that passes through Pluto's atmosphere would be refracted. *Refraction* is the bending of light rays as they change from one material into another, such as from a liquid into a gas.

Earth's atmosphere consists of several gases, including nitrogen, oxygen, and carbon dioxide. Each of these gases is made up of very tiny particles called *molecules*. Scientists suspected that if Pluto had an atmosphere, it would contain far fewer gas molecules in a given volume. In others words, Pluto's atmosphere was expected to be far less dense than Earth's. *Density* is a measurement of how much mass there is in a given volume.

Scientists use the term *atmospheric pressure* when referring to an atmosphere's density. The gases in the atmosphere are constantly moving, pushing against things and therefore creating pressure. The more gases there are in a given volume, the higher the atmospheric pressure. Based on their calculations, scientists knew that even if Pluto had an atmosphere with a pressure a million times less than that of Earth's, they could still detect it. All they had to do was get a clear look at Pluto as it passed in front of a star that was giving off enough light. If Pluto had an atmosphere, the light from the star would be refracted as it passed through the gases in Pluto's atmosphere and into the near-vacuum of space where there are no gas molecules.

In 1985, Pluto did pass in front of such a star. Unfortunately, the best places on Earth to view this eclipse were from areas covered by an ocean. Obviously, this was impossible. The next best place was in the Middle East. So that year, two scientists in Israel set their sights on Pluto. The images they obtained showed that the star's light was being refracted. Pluto seemed to have an atmosphere. However, there was a problem with the images. At that time, Israel was fighting an air war in Lebanon. The night sky was filled with light coming from artillery guns and rockets fired from jets. All this light affected the images and made it impossible for the scientists to reach a definite conclusion. The question of whether Pluto had an atmosphere was still open to debate.

Then in 1988 came another opportunity to observe Pluto eclipse a star. This time the best places to view it from Earth were in Australia and New Zealand. This was still a large area, and no one could predict exactly where the best viewing spot would be. So scientists in seven different observatories stretching across these two countries focused their telescopes on Pluto. Still, something was bothering the scientists.

They knew that even if it were a clear night, Earth's atmosphere would still interfere with what little light came from the star that Pluto was about to eclipse. The only way to avoid this problem was to look at the eclipse from a point as far above Earth's atmosphere as possible. To get the best view possible of the eclipse, several scientists asked to borrow a telescope from the National Aeronautics and Space Administration (NASA). This telescope was quite large. In addition, it was equipped with a CCD that had been especially designed for studying eclipses. But what was most important is that the telescope was not on Earth. It was carried by a converted military cargo jet. Known as the Kuiper Airborne Observatory, the telescope could produce images of

For many years, the Kuiper Airborne Observatory was the world's only airborne astronomical facility. Kuiper allowed scientists to make astronomical observations from anywhere within Earth's atmosphere with freedom from cloud cover.

Pluto taken from more than 40,000 feet (12,000 m) above Earth. These images would be clearer than any taken from Earth because at that altitude there would be far less atmospheric interference of the light coming from Pluto.

Pluto's Atmosphere

In 1988, this airborne telescope discovered that Pluto does have an atmosphere. The images taken by this telescope also revealed some details about Pluto's atmosphere. It is very different from any of the other planets. Some planets, like Earth, have a dense atmosphere that is mostly packed into a layer several miles thick and close to the surface. In contrast, Pluto's atmosphere is very thin and stretches for thousands of miles into space.

In 1992, scientists discovered that in addition to methane, Pluto's atmosphere also contains nitrogen and carbon monoxide. They also calculated that its atmosphere is made mostly of nitrogen, with only small amounts of carbon monoxide and methane. Earth's atmosphere is also made mostly of nitrogen. Fortunately, however, Earth's atmosphere contains far less carbon monoxide and methane than Pluto's. If it didn't, very few things that currently live on Earth could survive.

The use of NASA's airborne telescope was not the first time that Pluto had been studied from space. In 1983, NASA and the European Space Agency launched the Infrared Astronomical Satellite (IRAS) into space. This satellite contained an instrument specifically designed to measure the surface temperatures of objects in space. Scientists calculated Pluto's surface temperature to be –377° F (–227° C).

In 1986, evidence was obtained that Pluto's surface was even colder, perhaps as cold as –390° F (–234° C). The difference in tem-

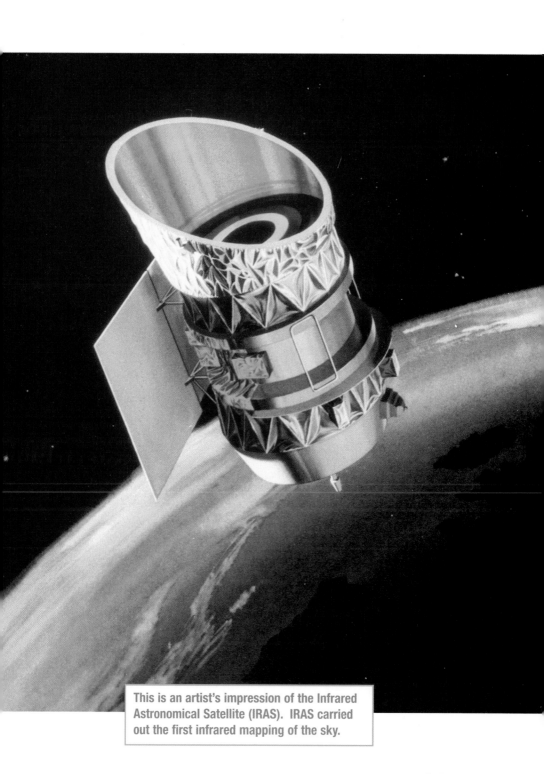

This is an artist's impression of the Infrared Astronomical Satellite (IRAS). IRAS carried out the first infrared mapping of the sky.

perature from the one measured in 1983 may seem insignificant. After all, both are extremely cold. Nothing could survive at these temperatures on Earth, where the lowest temperature ever recorded is −129° F (−89° C). But scientists still wondered—how truly cold is Pluto?

The temperature measurements obtained in 1983 and in 1986 both appear to be correct. Scientists think that Pluto has some surface areas that are colder than others. These colder regions are near its poles and are thought to be covered mostly with nitrogen ice. The warmer regions are found between the poles and are thought to have less nitrogen ice.

The Hubble Space Telescope

This conclusion about Pluto's colder and warmer regions is supported by images taken in 1994 with the *Hubble Space Telescope* (*HST*). The *HST* was launched into space on April 24, 1990, aboard the space shuttle *Discovery*. The *HST* was released from the shuttle two days later and went into an orbit about 370 miles (600 km) above Earth. Equipped with a variety of instruments, the *HST* was designed to take a closer look into deep space. Like the Kuiper Airborne Observatory, the *HST* orbits above Earth's atmosphere where it can take clearer images.

In 1994, the *HST* sent images of nearly the entire surface of Pluto back to Earth. These images revealed a darker central region and two brighter polar caps. The contrast between the light and dark areas was quite striking. In fact, scientists have never observed such contrasts on any other planet, except Earth. Just what this means will not be known until closer and clearer images of Pluto are obtained. But even for the *HST*, picking up any surface detail on Pluto is like spotting a baseball at a distance of 40 miles (65 km).

Technology at Work: Fixing the HST

After being repaired four times, the *HST* again needed some repair work in 2002. On February 28, the space shuttle *Columbia* was launched on a twelve-day mission. One of its main goals was to fix and upgrade the *HST*. During its space voyage, *Columbia* docked with the *HST* and attached it to a brace in its open cargo bay. Four astronauts working in pairs took five space walks to work on the *HST*. Each space walk lasted six to seven hours.

One space walk was spent on removing the last of the *HST*'s original instruments, a camera, and replacing it with one called the Advanced Camera for Surveys. About the size of a telephone booth, the new camera weighs about 800 pounds (350 kilograms) and will enable the *HST* to take an even closer look into space. Another space walk replaced one of the telescope's devices that controls its movement as it turns from one target to another. In all, the astronauts installed some 6,000 pounds (2,700 kg) of equipment on the *HST*. After the astronauts completed their work, the space shuttle used its robot arm to place the *HST* back in its orbit.

This was the fifth space shuttle mission sent to keep the *HST* in working order. The next, and last, is scheduled for 2004 to make the final updates and correct any problems so that the *HST* can complete its twenty-year mission in 2010, and perhaps take more images of Pluto.

Astronauts James H. Newman (on *Columbia*'s Remote Manipulator System) and Michael Massimino removed the Faint Object Camera to make room for the new Advanced Camera for Surveys.

The fastest route to Pluto and Charon is not a direct path from Earth. Even though the Pluto spacecraft will be nuclear-powered, it would take too long to fly directly from Earth to the double planet. Instead, the craft will be launched so that it meets up with Jupiter sometime in 2007. As the spacecraft approaches Jupiter, gravity will pull it into orbit around the planet. As Jupiter continues to orbit the Sun, the craft will get help from the planet's immense gravity. Jupiter's gravity will help "slingshot" the spacecraft to speeds up to 50,000 mph (80,000 kph) to continue its trip to Pluto and Charon. Using a planet's gravity and the velocity of its orbit around the Sun to speed up a spacecraft is known as gravity-assist.

Scientists hope that the craft will use a camera equipped with a long-range telephoto lens to start looking at Pluto and Charon when it is about 100,000 miles (160,000 km) away from them. If Pluto's atmosphere does freeze and thaw, this would be the best chance to view this change. The closest the craft will get to Pluto is 6,000 miles (10,000 km) and to Charon is 17,000 miles (27,000 km). The spacecraft will be this close for one Earth day. Any surface features as small as 200 feet (60 m) across will be seen.

Scientists will also start sending signals to the spacecraft. Instruments onboard the craft will measure how these signals are affected by Pluto's atmosphere. These measurements will provide information on the composition, temperature, and density of the gases in Pluto's atmosphere. Even after passing by the double planet, the spacecraft's camera will still be looking at Pluto and Charon to examine their mostly dark side and to look for rings.

In 1996, the instruments on the *HST* were again pointed toward Pluto. These images revealed a little more detail about Pluto's surface, even though the planet was still 3 billion miles (4.8 billion km) from Earth. They showed twelve major regions on Pluto, each with its own distinct brightness. These bright and dark regions may indicate that large fields of nitrogen and methane ice shift on Pluto's surface as it orbits the Sun. What was also interesting was a cluster of dark spots that the *HST* detected. These may be basins and craters, just like on our Moon.

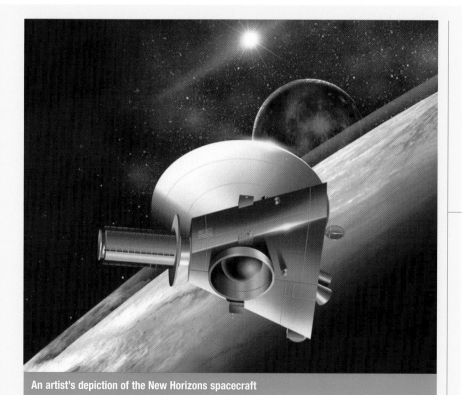
An artist's depiction of the New Horizons spacecraft

At about the same time that the *HST* was looking at Pluto, another satellite was also aimed at the planet. This was the Infrared Space Observatory (ISO) that was launched in 1995. One of the ISO's missions was to measure the temperature of Pluto's surface. Measurements revealed that some places on Pluto are even colder than scientists had thought. The colder temperatures correspond to the bright areas that the *HST* had detected. Here the lowest temperature was measured at –396° F (–238° C). The warmer temperatures correspond to the dark regions seen on Pluto's surface. Some of the dark regions were as warm as −342° F (−208° C). Scientists expected that the darker regions would be warmer than the brighter regions. The darker a material is, the more sunlight it absorbs. The more sunlight it absorbs, the warmer it gets.

One thing scientists want to know is how the surface temperature of Pluto changes as the planet orbits the Sun. Unfortunately, the ISO was not able to provide any information after 1998. In May of that year, it reached its life expectancy and burned up in the atmosphere as it fell back to Earth. Scientists, however, were not too disappointed. NASA was planning to launch a spacecraft to Pluto and Charon that they hoped would provide much more information about the double planet. The mission was appropriately called the Pluto Fast Flyby.

Taking a Close Look

Much has been learned about the planets from spacecraft that fly by them as closely as possible. In 1979, *Voyager 1* and *Voyager 2* approached Jupiter, the planet in the outer solar system closest to the Sun. These spacecraft detected a series of rings that circled the planet. They even captured images of active volcanoes on one of Jupiter's moons. Spacecraft have also been launched to land on planets. In 1998, the *Mars Global Surveyor* sent back pictures of the planet's polar ice cap. Being the farthest from Earth, Pluto would obviously be the last planet on NASA's list to be the target of a flyby mission. But NASA would eventually get around to planning and scheduling a mission to Pluto. The launch date was set for sometime in 2001.

Unfortunately, the funds to design and build the Pluto Fast Flyby spacecraft were cut from NASA's budget. Obviously, the spacecraft never took off in 2001. However, NASA is involved in a new project, called New Horizons, which is designed to launch a spacecraft to Pluto and Charon in January 2006. The spacecraft is scheduled to arrive at the double planet as early as 2015, before Pluto enters the part of its orbit that takes it too far from the Sun. If the spacecraft is launched and flies by Pluto and Charon closely enough, scientists hope to learn much more about their surface features and atmosphere. They may also get the information they need to answer a question that some scientists have asked: is Pluto really a planet?

This is an artist's depiction of a Kuiper Belt object. In this case, the object is known as a binary object, which means it orbits the Sun in tandem with another object (the dark, round object in background). It takes the two 301 years to orbit the Sun.

Chapter 7

The Debate

When Clyde Tombaugh discovered Pluto in 1930, another planet was added to our solar system, bringing the total to nine. When the American Museum of National History in New York City opened its Rose Center for Earth and Space in 2000, only eight planets were on display. Pluto was not among them. The astronomers at the museum had decided that Pluto did not meet the criteria of being a planet. Instead, the astronomers at the Rose Center classify Pluto as one of many icy objects whose orbit lies beyond Neptune. This region of space is called the Kuiper Belt.

In 1992, scientists found the first object in the Kuiper Belt. Since then, they have spotted at least seventy thousand other objects in this region. All these objects are small chunks of rock and ice hurling through space. Most measure between 60 and 300 miles (100 and 500 km) in diameter. Many of them travel in orbits similar to Pluto's. These objects go by several names, including Plutinos, Kuiper Belt Objects (KBOs), and Trans-Neptunian Objects (TNOs).

Of all the planetariums in the United States, only the Rose Center considers Pluto to not be a planet, but rather a Plutino, KBO, or TNO. A display of our solar system at the planetarium includes a description that reads, "Beyond the outer planets is the Kuiper Belt of comets, a disk of small, icy worlds including Pluto."

The Rose Center does not list Pluto as a planet in its Scales of the Universe exhibit.

Gerard Kuiper and the KBOs

The existence of the Kuiper Belt was first proposed by scientists in the 1980s to explain the origin of comets known as short-period comets. These comets complete their orbits around the Sun in less than two hundred years, as opposed to long-period comets, which take much longer. One of the most famous short-period comets is Halley's Comet.

The scientists calculated that short-period comets could not have originated from a region in space known as the Oort cloud, which was known to be a source of comets. They predicted that a second source of comets must exist, which became known as the Kuiper Belt, named in honor of Gerard Kuiper, a Dutch-American planetary scientist who lived from 1905 to 1973. Among Kuiper's many accomplishments was his prediction of icy bodies orbiting the Sun just beyond Pluto in the region of space now bearing his name.

The first KBO was spotted in 1992. In 2000, a rather large KBO was discovered. Named Varuna, this KBO has a diameter of about 560 miles (900 km). Using the Keck I and Keck II telescopes in Hawaii, astronomers calculated Varuna's albedo to be 7 percent, making it much darker than both Pluto and Charon. At the time, Varuna's diameter made it the second-largest known asteroid, behind Ceres. In 2001, an even larger KBO was spotted with the help of a 158-inch (4-m) telescope.

Dubbed 2001 KX76, this larger KBO is thought to have a diameter of 788 miles (1,268 km), making it larger than Ceres and even Charon. Interestingly, images of 2001 KX76 have since been found dating as far back as 1982. The discovery of this largest known KBO has prompted scientists to speculate that many large KBOs, perhaps even larger than 2001 KX76, remain to be discovered. In fact, they think that KBOs as large or even larger than Pluto are waiting to be spotted.

Gerard Kuiper predicted the existence of Kuiper Belt objects.

Many visitors to the Rose Center ask why Pluto is no longer considered a planet. To understand both sides of this debate, you must first recognize that the definition of a planet is not very precise. Most people consider any object in space to be a planet if it meets two criteria. First, it must directly orbit the Sun or another star and not another object in space. This is why our Moon is not a planet. Although our Moon orbits the Sun, it does so indirectly while it orbits Earth. Second, the object must be big enough so that its gravity pulls it together to form a round sphere.

Pluto meets both these criteria. Although its orbit is unusual, Pluto does travel around the Sun. Although little is known about its surface, we do know that is spherical. Everyone agrees that Pluto then meets this rather loose definition of a planet. Then why do some scientists not consider it a planet?

The Nebular Hypothesis

The reason is based on how our solar system originated. Over the years, scientists have suggested a number of hypotheses as to how the planets were formed. Scientists think that our solar system was formed from a slowly spinning cloud made mostly of gases with some dust. This cloud of gases and dust is known as a *nebula*. For obvious reasons, this is known as the nebular hypothesis. According to this hypothesis, the nebula started to collapse under its own *weight*, with gravity pulling all the gas and dust toward the center. As the dust and gases began to come together, the nebula spun faster and faster. As material fell inward it was converted to heat. The temperature at the center rose until a ball of glowing gas was formed.

The temperature at the center of this ball became so great that a process called *nuclear fusion* started. Nuclear fusion occurs when the nuclei of atoms combine to form a different element. In this case, atoms of hydrogen gas combined to form atoms of helium. In the process, huge amounts of energy were released. This is how our Sun is believed to have formed. To this day, nuclear fusion is still occurring in our Sun.

Not all the material in the nebula formed the Sun. Some of the gases and dust continued to orbit around the Sun as it was forming. Some of this material started clumping together. These clumps grew bigger and bigger as more and more particles were pulled in by gravity. The dust in these areas started to stick together to form larger and larger dust balls. Slowly, the nebula formed many *planetesimals*, which represent the first stage in the formation of a planet. At first, a planetesimal is only a few miles or kilometers in diameter. But other planetesimals may collide with it. The collision might break up the planetesimals into even smaller fragments. It might also knock the planetesimals out of their orbits. However, the collision might also cause the planetesimals to join and become one larger mass. When the mass gets large enough, then a planet is born. Forming a planet from a nebula took between one and one hundred million years.

Scientists have made observations that support the nebular hypothesis. They have observed young stars similar to our Sun forming in nebulae swirling in space. Additional evidence comes from asteroids, comets, and *meteoroids*. A meteoroid is a small rocky or metallic object floating in space. Asteroids, comets, and meteoroids are all examples of small bodies in our solar system that failed to join planetesimals in becoming a planet.

...posite image shows the four
.. planets of the outer solar system.

According to the nebular hypothesis, several planets formed near the Sun. These include Mercury, Venus, Earth, and Mars, the four planets of the inner solar system. These four planets are composed mostly of rocks and metals that came from the solid dusty materials in the nebula. Because these four planets are closest to the Sun, the solar heat drove most of the lighter gases, such as hydrogen and helium, into the outer solar system.

The nebula hypothesis also states that several planets formed farther away from the sun. These include Jupiter, Saturn, Uranus, and Neptune, the four planets of the outer solar system. Because these

planets are farther away from the Sun, the hydrogen and helium gases did not get driven away by solar heat. As a result, these four outer planets contain lots of hydrogen and helium gases, unlike the four inner planets.

A Planet Unlike the Others

Those who no longer consider Pluto a planet point out that it is very different from both the inner and outer planets. Pluto is not rocky like the inner planets. This is not unexpected as the planet is so far from the Sun. However, Pluto is also not like the outer planets. Information obtained so far indicates that Pluto is made mostly of nitrogen and methane ice, very different from the hydrogen and helium gases that make up the four outer planets. Those who still consider Pluto a planet suggest that much still remains to be learned about the composition of Pluto. Perhaps the New Horizons mission will reveal that Pluto is more like the four outer planets than we first thought.

But those who claim that Pluto is not a planet point to other evidence to support their view. The four outer planets are all rather large. Jupiter, for example, has a volume that is fourteen hundred times larger than Earth. Compared to the other planets in the outer solar system, Pluto is a dwarf. In fact, Pluto is far smaller than any of the planets in the inner solar system. Seven of the moons in our solar system are even bigger than Pluto. Some people say that Pluto is just too small to be considered a planet. In response, Pluto's supporters say that Pluto is still too big to be considered a comet or some other nonplanetary object in space. These supporters point to Ceres, an asteroid found in the belt between Mars and Jupiter. Ceres, the largest nonplanetary object in space, is some 600 miles (1,000 km) across. Pluto is some three times larger.

Ceres, however, is also used as an example by those who no longer consider Pluto a planet. Ceres was first observed in 1801. At that time, astronomers called it a planet. But then they soon started discovering other smaller, rocky objects in the same belt between Mars and Jupiter. A year after its discovery, Ceres was no longer considered a planet but one of many asteroids that travel in this belt. If Ceres can be reclassified, some say, so can Pluto. In response, Pluto's supporters point out that Ceres was considered a planet for only one year. Pluto was called a planet for nearly seventy years before scientists began to question whether it was a planet. Tradition, Pluto's supporters argue, is on their side.

Ceres (marked by the arrow) was once considered a planet.

In addition to its icy composition and very small size, those who say Pluto is not a planet point to its unusual orbit. Recall that Pluto's orbit is an ellipse, like those of all the other planets. But Pluto's orbit is the only one that is significantly tilted from all the others. Moreover, Pluto's orbit is extremely eccentric, meaning that its ellipse is very elongated. As a result, Pluto's orbit takes it inside Neptune's during 20 years of its 248-year orbit. There are a number of other objects in the Kuiper Belt whose orbits are like Pluto's. Therefore, some argue that Pluto's orbit is another reason why it is not a planet. But those who say that Pluto is a planet point out that the definition of a planet says nothing about how an object in space has to orbit the Sun.

Definition of a Planet

Perhaps the question about Pluto's status in our solar system can be answered if the definition of the word "planet" is made more specific. The word "planet" originally meant "wanderer." So anything that wanders or moves through space is a planet. Thus, everything in our solar system, except the Sun, can be considered a planet according to this definition. Scientists quickly realized that a planet could not be defined this way. The rather vague definition used today is not much more help. Pluto is a sphere that orbits the Sun. But so are many thousands of other objects in space orbiting the Sun, especially in the Kuiper Belt where Pluto is found.

Scientists still have not agreed on a more specific definition of a planet. However, two proposals have been made. One is "a non-moon, Sun-orbiting body large enough to have gravitationally pulled itself into a roughly spherical shape." If this definition is accepted, then

Pluto will remain a planet. But several asteroids, including Ceres, also fit this definition. Will the number of planets in our solar system then rise dramatically?

Another proposed definition of a planet is "a non-moon, sun-orbiting body large enough to have gravitationally 'swept out' almost everything else near its orbit." The term "swept out" refers to a planet clearing the space around it by pulling in all the smaller bodies near it. Based on this definition, Pluto would not be a planet, as it has not cleared the area near it of the Kuiper Belt comets.

The official position of Pluto's status will undoubtedly be affected by how the International Astronomical Union (IAU) defines a planet. As the organization's names implies, this is a worldwide association of scientists. The IAU has more than eight thousand members from more than eighty countries. In 1999, the IAU issued this statement: "No proposal to change the status of Pluto as the ninth planet in the solar system has been made by . . . the IAU." The announcement went on to say, "Ways to classify planets by physical characteristics are also under consideration. These discussions are continuing and will take some time." No one knows when the IAU will issue its definition of a planet.

Our Solar System

According to the nebular hypothesis, all the objects in our solar system formed from a cloud of gases and dust. The Sun and the planets of the outer solar system, with the exception of Pluto, formed as the materials in the nebula condensed because of gravity. The planets of the inner solar system formed as planetesimals collided and joined together to form bigger and bigger masses, including the larger moons such as our own. Much of the materials in the nebula that did not form the Sun, a planet, or a larger moon formed KBOs, asteroids, smaller moons, comets, and meteoroids. In effect, our solar system is made up of objects that represent a wide range of sizes and composition—from tiny comets to large planets—all created from the same source.

In view of the origin of our solar system, scientists point out that deciding if an object in space is a planet is not as straightforward as it may seem. The dividing line between a small planet and a large comet or asteroid is vague. Remember that Ceres, now classified as an asteroid, was considered a planet when it was first discovered in 1800.

Whether Pluto is a planet may be debated for some time to come. But there is no argument about a number of facts concerning Pluto. Pluto orbits the Sun in an unusual elliptical path. In turn, Pluto is orbited by its moon, Charon. Pluto takes 6.39 days to complete one rotation on its axis and 248 Earth years to complete one orbit around the Sun. Pluto has a thin atmosphere containing methane, nitrogen, and carbon monoxide and a surface made of methane ice. But much more remains to be learned about Pluto. Scientists hope that the New Horizons project will answer their questions. Getting a close look at Pluto and KBOs may provide scientists with insight as to what happened when objects in our solar system were formed from a nebula. These distant icy objects are thought to consist of material left over from the creation of our solar system.

When Tombaugh discovered Pluto in 1930, he and other astronomers believed that they had found Planet X. With the addition of this ninth planet to our solar system, they felt that Neptune's orbit could be explained. However, when Pluto turned out to be so small in both size and mass, scientists were confused. They knew that Pluto's small mass meant that its gravity was not strong enough to account for Neptune's orbit. Today, scientists realize that these astronomers were wrong. Neptune's orbit, like that of Uranus, is not unusual at all. There was never any reason to suggest that Planet X existed. If Tombaugh had known this, he may never have searched for Pluto.

Comparing
Pluto to Earth

Vital Statistics

	Pluto	Earth	Pluto/Earth Ratio
MASS	1.3×10^{22} kg	5.97×10^{24} kg	0.0022
VOLUME	6.4×10^{9} km^3	1.08×10^{12} km^3	0.0059
DENSITY	2.03 g/cm^3	5.515 g/cm^3	0.368
RADIUS	1,150 km	6,378 km	0.18
OBLATENESS	0.02293	0.000335	6.84
AVERAGE ORBITAL VELOCITY	4.74 km/s	29.78 km/s	0.159
ORBITAL PERIOD	90.570 days	365.2 days	248
LENGTH OF DAY	153.36 hours	24 hours	6.39
AXIAL TILT	119.6 degrees	23.45 degrees	5.1
PERIHELION	4.5×109 km	1.47×108 km	30.6
APHELION	7.4×10^{9} km	1.52×10^{8} km	48.7
AVERAGE DISTANCE FROM THE SUN	5.93×10^{9} km	1.5×10^{8} km	39.5
NUMBER OF SATELLITES	1	1	
RING SYSTEM	no	no	
MAGNETOSPHERE	unknown	yes	
AVERAGE TEMPERATURE	–390°F (–234°C)	59°F (15°C)	

Exploring Pluto: A Timeline

1846 — One week after Neptune is discovered, an astronomer proposes that there still may be another planet out there.

1877 — David Todd fails in his attempt to spot this ninth planet.

1905 — Percival Lowell proposes the name Planet X. His search for this planet continues without any success until his death in 1916.

1930 — Clyde Tombaugh discovers Planet X and names it Pluto. The Lowell Observatory describes Pluto's orbit.

1954 — Pluto is discovered to take 6.39 days to rotate once.

1965 — Pluto is discovered to orbit the Sun twice for every three orbits made by Neptune.

1976 — Methane ice is discovered on Pluto's surface.

1978 — James Christy discovers Pluto's only moon and names it Charon.

1985-91	—	Eclipses between Pluto and Charon provide scientists with opportunities to learn more about the double planet, including more precise measurements of their size and mass.
1988	—	Images conclusively reveal that Pluto has an atmosphere.
1992	—	Nitrogen and carbon monoxide are discovered on Pluto.
1994	—	The Hubble Space Telescope begins providing clearer images of Pluto and Charon.
1996	—	Images from the Hubble Space Telescope suggest Pluto may have basins and craters.
2000	—	The Rose Center for Earth and Space does not include Pluto among its list of planets.
2001	—	The Pluto Fast Flyby mission to get a close view of the planet is canceled.
2006	—	NASA plans to launch the New Horizons mission to Pluto.
2015	—	The New Horizons spacecraft should arrive at Pluto and Charon.

Glossary

albedo—the measurement of the percentage of sunlight reflected by an object in outer space

asteroid—a large rock that orbits the Sun

astronomer—a scientist who studies objects and forces acting in space

atmospheric pressure—the force exerted by the atmosphere

central event—a total eclipse seen from Earth that occurs when one body in space passes completely in front of another body

charged-coupled device (CCD)—a digital camera that translates millions of electrical charges into an image

comet—a ball of rock and ice that travels around the Sun from the outer edges of the solar system

density—the amount of matter present in a given space, usually expressed in grams per cubic centimeter

diameter—the distance between two points on the edge of a circle through its center *eclipse*—the passage of one object in front of another object so as to either partially or completely block it from view

element—a building block of matter

ellipse—an elongated, or somewhat flattened, circle

gravity—the force of attraction between two objects that depends on their masses and the distance between them

hypothesis—an educated guess made by a scientist

inner solar system—the region of space that includes Mercury, Venus, Earth, our Moon, Mars, and the Asteroid Belt

Kuiper Belt—the region in space beyond the orbit of Neptune where certain comets originate

mass—the amount of matter that an object has, usually expressed in grams or kilograms

meteoroid—a small rocky or metallic object floating in space

molecule—a particle that makes up certain substances, such as water, oxygen, and methane ice

mutual event—a partial eclipse seen from Earth that occurs when one body in space passes in front of another body

nebula—a cloud of gases and dust in space that can form a star or planet

nuclear fusion—the process when the nuclei of atoms combine to form atoms of a new element

outer solar system—the region of space that includes Jupiter, Saturn, Uranus, Neptune, Pluto, and the Kuiper Belt

parallax—the apparent movement of an object when viewed from two different positions

photomultiplier tube (PMT)—a device that multiplies or amplifies a light signal it receives

planetesimal—a solid object formed by gas and dust in a nebula that may combine with other planetisimals to form a planet

refraction—the bending of light rays as they pass from one material into another, such as from air into water

satellite—a natural or human-made object that orbits another object in space, such as a planet

spectrograph—a device that is used to study the electromagnetic radiation of an object and that records the object's spectrum (distribution of electromagnetic radiation)

volume—the amount of space an object occupies

weight—the measurement of the gravitational attraction for a particular mass

To Find Out More

The news from space changes fast, so it's always a good idea to check the copyright date on books, CD-ROMs, and videotapes to make sure that you are getting up-to-date information. One good place to look for current information from NASA is U.S. government depository libraries. There are several in each state.

Books

Bredeson, Carmen. *Pluto*. Danbury, Conn.: Franklin Watts, 2000.

Brimmer, Larry Dane. *Pluto*. Danbury, Conn: Children's Press, 1999.

Stern, Alan, and Jacqueline Mitton. *Pluto and Charon: Ice Worlds on the Ragged Edge of the Solar System*. New York: John Wiley & Sons, 1997.

Thompson, Luke. *Pluto*. New York: Powerkids Press, 2001.

Vogt, Gregory L. *Pluto*. Mankato, Minn.: Bridgestone Books, 2000.

———— *Pluto and the Search for New Planets*. Austin, Tex.: Raintree Steck-Vaughn Publishers, 2000.

Wetterer, Margaret K., and Laurie A. Caple. *Clyde Tombaugh and the Search for Planet X*. Minneapolis: Carolrhoda Books, 1996.

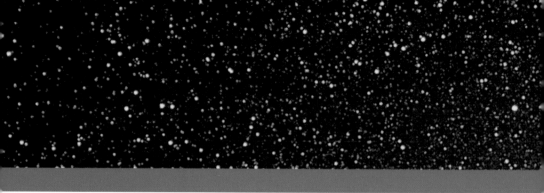

Organizations and Online Sites

Several of the websites listed here are NASA sites, with links to many other interesting sources of information about Pluto and the other planets of the solar system. You can also sign up to receive NASA news on many subjects via e-mail.

Lowell Observatory
http://www.lowell.edu
The observatory where Clyde Tombaugh first spotted Pluto still operates. Its website has an online educational section.

NASA Jet Propulsion Laboratory
http://www.jpl.nasa.gov
Click on "Solar System" and then on "Welcome to the Planets." At this site, you can see the best images from NASA's planetary exploration program, including those taken of Pluto by the *HST*.

http://pds.jpl.nasa.gov/planets/welcome/pluto.htm
Check out NASA's latest facts about Pluto and the clearest view of Pluto and Charon as seen from the HST.

http://www.jpl.nasa.gov/ice_fire/edout.htm
This is the site for any student who is interested in becoming involved in the Pluto-Kuiper Express. You can click the links to find

out more about the design of the spacecraft and the instruments it will probably carry.

The Planet Pluto

http://the-planet-pluto.com/

Check out some photographs of Pluto and Charon. You can also find out how much you learned from this book by taking a fifteen-question multiple-choice quiz.

The Planetary Society

http://planetary.org/

65 North Catalina Avenue

Pasadena, CA 91106-2301

Among the many links, you can find one that provides a list of space-related events from around the world.

Pluto Home Page

http://dosxx.colorado.edu/plutohome.html

Get all the facts about Pluto and Charon. Links will take you to sites where you can get additional information, including an update on the Pluto-Kuiper Express.

Pluto: Planet or Comet?

http://news.nationalgeographic.com/news/2001/02/0216_Pluto.html

Read more about the debate as to whether or not Pluto is a planet.

Princeton Planetary Society
http://.princeton.edu/~space
This site has a student organization for anyone interested in astronomy or space-related topics. You can be added to the mailing list by writing to space@princeton.edu.

Sky Online
http://www.skyandtelescope.com/
This is the website for *Sky & Telescope* magazine where you can find a weekly news section on space-related topics. You can also find tips for amateur astronomers. A list of science museums, planetariums, and astronomy clubs organized by state can help you find nearby places to visit.

Places to Visit

Check the Internet (*www.skypub.com* is a good place to start), your local visitor's center, or your phone directory for planetariums and science museums near you. Here are a few suggestions.

American Museum of Natural History
Rose Center for Earth and Space
Central Park West at 79th Street
New York, NY 10024-5192
http://amnh.org/rose/
At this site, you can check out the floor plans and show times and take a peek at the displays to get an idea of what you can see during

your visit. Keep in mind that there is one thing you will not see here—a model of Pluto in the display of our solar system.

Exploratorium
3601 Lyon Street
San Francisco, CA 94123
http://www.exploratorium.edu
This science center features interactive exhibits, including space-related subjects.

NASA Jet Propulsion Laboratory
4800 Oak Grove Drive
Pasadena, CA 91109
http://jpl.nasa.gov
This lab is the primary center for all NASA planetary missions. Scientists working here are presently developing plans for the New Horizons mission. To arrange a visit, click on "Education" and then on "NASA Education Links."

National Air and Space Museum
7th and Independence Avenue, S.W.
Washington, DC 20560
http://nasm.ed/nasm/planetarium
Visit the Albert Einstein Planetarium, where you can tour our universe through images projected on its 70-foot (21-m)-diameter dome.

About the Author

Salvatore Tocci taught high school and college science for almost 30 years. He has a B.A. degree from Cornell University and a Master of Philosophy degree from The City University of New York.

He has written books that deal with a range of science topics, from biographies of famous scientists to a high school chemistry text. He has also traveled throughout the United States to present workshops at national science conventions to show teachers how to emphasize the applications of scientific knowledge in our everyday lives.

Mr. Tocci lives in East Hampton, New York, with his wife, Patti. Both retired from teaching, they spend their leisure time sailing and traveling. On a recent trip to Florida, they went to Cape Canaveral to see a shuttle launch. Unfortunately, it was postponed.

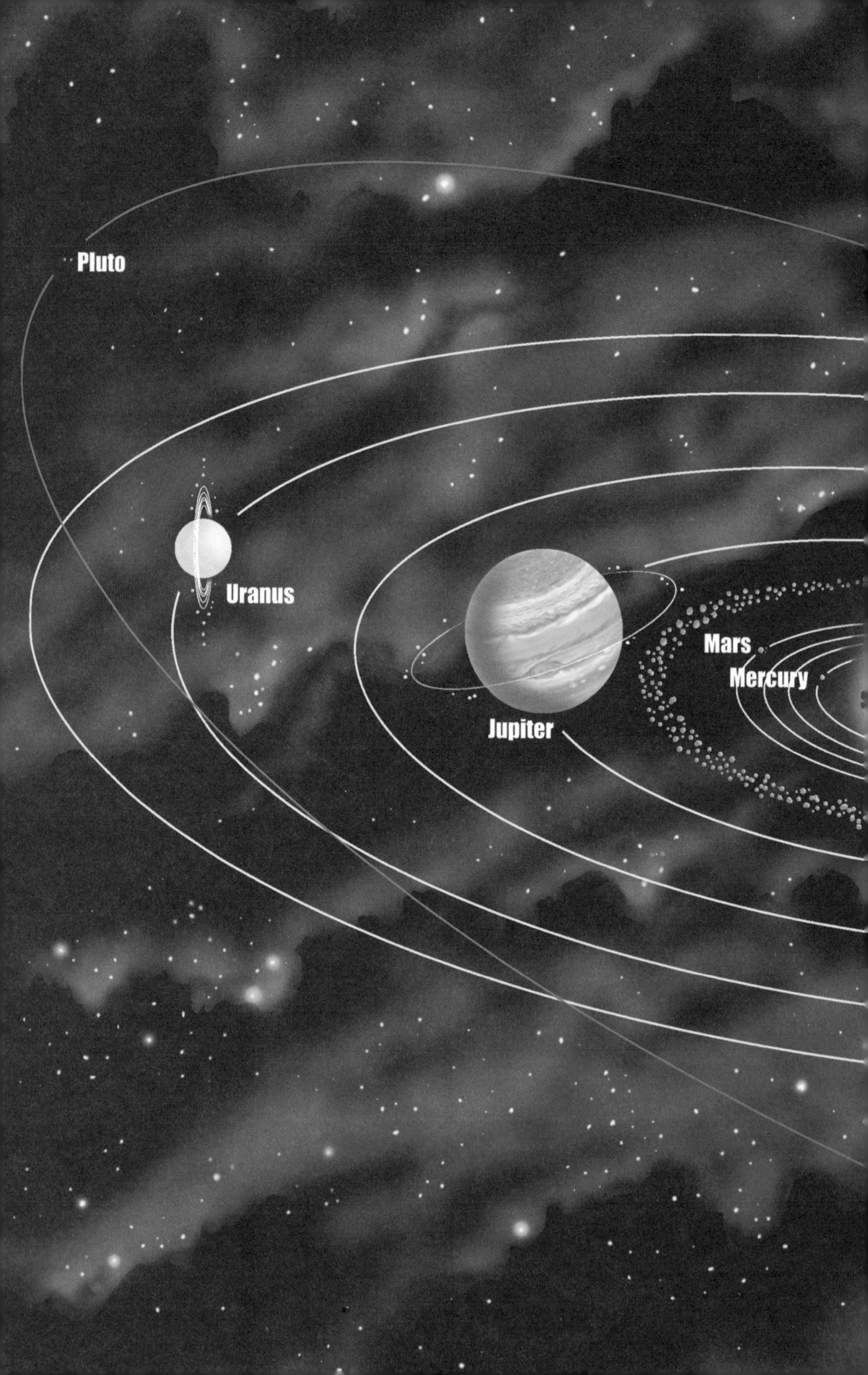

Pluto
Uranus
Jupiter
Mars
Mercury